What Did the Buddha Really Teach?

Dhammapada

Dhammapada- A collection of Gautama Buddha's verses from the Pali Canon Translated into English from the Sinhala Translation

By Venerable Kiribathgoda Gnanananda Thera

A Mahamegha Publication

What Does the Buddha Really Teach?

Dhammapada- A collection of Gautama Buddha's verses from the Pali Canon Translated into English from the Sinhala Translation By Venerable Kiribathgoda Gnanananda Thera

2016 All Rights Reserved
ISBN: 978-1536813036
Published July 2016

Computer Typesetting by
Buddha Meditation Centre- Greater Toronto
Markham, Ontario, Canada L6C 1P2
Telephone: 905-927-7117
www.meditationgta.org

Published by

Mahamegha Publishers

Waduwawa, Yatigaloluwa, Polgahawela,
Sri Lanka.
Telephone: +037 2053300, 076 8255703
mahameghapublishers@gmail.com

Namo Tassa Bhagavato Arahato Sammā Sambuddhassa!

Homage to the Blessed One,
the Worthy One,
the Supremely Enlightened One!

Contents

PREFACE	6
1. PAIRS	17
2. DILIGENCE	21
3. THE MIND	24
4. FLOWERS	26
5. THE FOOL	29
6. THE WISE	32
7. THE LIBERATED ONE	35
8. THE THOUSANDS	38
9. EVIL	41
10. VIOLENCE	44
11. OLD AGE	47
12. ONESELF	50
13. THE WORLD	52
14. THE BUDDHA	54

Table of Contents

15. HAPPINESS	**58**
16. THE DEAR	**60**
17. ANGER	**62**
18. STAIN	**65**
19. ON DHAMMA	**69**
20. THE PATH	**72**
21. MISCELLANEOUS	**76**
22. HELL	**79**
23. THE KING ELEPHANT	**82**
24. CRAVING	**85**
25. THE MONK	**91**
26. THE TRUE BRĀHMIN	**96**

PREFACE

The Great Teacher, Supreme Buddha, has taught the beautiful Dhamma out of limitless compassion for all the beings. All the teachings taught by the Buddha are known as the message of the Great Teacher. The Buddha's message contains nine categories of teachings. They are as follows: 1. Discourses (Sutta) 2. Discourses mixed with verses (Geyya) 3. Discourses from the higher teachings without the verses (Veyyākarana) 4. Verses (Gathā) 5. Verses of inspired utterances (Udāna) 6. The 112 discourses which begins with the phrase "Thus the Blessed One has said" (Itivuttaka) 7. The 547 birth stories related by the Buddha in connection with his previous births (Jātaka) 8. The discourses that deal with the wonderful and the marvelous (Abbhūtadhamma) 9. Discourses of questions and answers (Vedalla).

The collection called the Dhammpada contains the verses (Gathā) uttered by the Buddha. These verses are called "The Message of Buddha" since they have an incredible quality.

Preface

Whoever understands the meaning of these verses and follows accordingly will have an amazing opportunity to achieve freedom from suffering, Nibbāna, and to experience true happiness.

One day, great Brahma Sahampati approached the Buddha and uttered a few verses about the noble qualities of the Buddha, the Dhamma, and the community of monks. In one of those verses, there is a remarkable statement: "Ekasmiṁ brahmacariyasmiṁ - sahassaṁ maccu hāyinaṁ" (SN:01) "A thousand enlightened monks who have defeated the evil-one dwell in a single word of the Dhamma."

You will witness the truth of this statement when you attentively study the verses in this book. "Dhammapada" is a mirror of that noble quality.

Dhammapada consists of twenty six chapters. These were categorized by specific topics by the great Arahants headed by the Great Arahant Mahā Kassapa Thero in the first Dhamma council. The skill of these Arahants of categorizing the incredible words of the Buddha into different topics is amazing.

The first chapter in this book is The Pairs (Yamaka Vaggo) which contains twenty verses. This chapter is made up of pairs of verses that were uttered at different locations by the Supreme Buddha. In this chapter, there are many meaningful teachings about life, mind, and the path to enlightenment. This is the beginning chapter of the Dhammapada.

What follows is the chapter on Diligence (Appamāda Vaggo). Here, diligence means a sense urgency of cultivating wholesome qualities. Effort to abandon unwholesomeness and to develop wholesomeness is aroused in one's life due to this diligence. Buddhas always praise diligence. By reading this chapter, you can learn the danger of negligence and the benefit of diligence through twelve beautiful verses.

The third chapter is on the Mind (Citta Vaggo). It has eleven awakening verses. The blessed one skillfully teaches the misery of a misled mind and the peace of a well guided mind.

The fourth chapter is on Flowers (Puppha Vaggo). You can learn sixteen verses taught by the Buddha, in which he used flowers as similes to describe life.

Next, you can read the chapter on the Fools (Bāla Vaggo). The fool in the Dhamma is described as an ordinary individual who does not understand the true meaning of merit/ demerit, grateful people/ungrateful people, right view/ wrong view, and right path/wrong path. You can learn about the lack of wisdom, arrogance, and ungratefulness of a fool by reading the sixteen verses in this chapter.

Next, the great Arahants selected fourteen elegant verses about the Wise (Pandita Vaggao). During Supreme Buddhas' time, when someone was addressed as the wise, they were referring to the enlightened monks. Through these verses, the Supreme Buddha shows us the value of the association of the wise and the integrity of the wise.

The seventh chapter consists of ten verses about the Enlightened Monk (Arahanta Vaggo). How wonderful it is to know about enlightened beings even in a time period like ours!

The eighth chapter is called the Thousands (Sahassa Vaggo). Dhamma facts on the theme of thousands and hundreds are presented in this chapter. You can learn the true meaning of a righteous living by reading this chapter.

All the Buddhas instruct both gods and humans to avoid sin. In the ninth chapter on the Evil (Pāpa Vaggo), you can learn thirteen verses about the true meaning of sin, its dangerous results, and how foolish people are attracted to evil.

The tenth chapter is on Violence (Danda Vaggo). Here, Buddha teaches how an ungrateful person deserves punishment all the way up to rebirth in hell. He also teaches about the feeling of peacefulness of a monk who avoids all evils. There are seventeen eye-opening verses in this chapter.

Deterioration as you age and the hardships that follow are detailed in the eleventh chapter about Old Age (Jarā Vagga). This chapter encompasses eleven verses. They explain how the intelligent noble disciple who follows the Noble Eightfold Path attains the freedom from old age and death through the understanding of the reality of life.

The twelfth chapter is on Oneself (Atta Vaggo). These ten verses teach you about the responsibility of taking care of oneself and protecting oneself. They highlight that the direction of life always depends on oneself.

The chapter on the World (Loka Vaggo) presents twelve verses about realizing the true nature of this world we call life.

The fourteenth chapter is on the Buddha (Buddha Vaggo). It contains eighteen verses. The extraordinary characteristics of the life of the Buddhas have been disclosed by the Gautama Buddha.

Everyone wants to be happy. The sole purpose of the appearance of a Buddha in the world is to teach the correct path to attain true happiness. Through the twelve verses in the chapter of Happiness (Sukha Vaggo), you can understand what happiness truly means.

Next, you can read the chapter on the Dear (Piya Vaggo). These twelve verses explain the dearest person in the world and how the beloved good kamma ripens.

Anger is a very dangerous defilement. To live with such a defilement is extremely dangerous. Therefore, through fourteen verses in the chapter on Anger (Kodha Vaggo), Buddha teaches practical techniques of overcoming anger.

Chapter eighteen is about Impurities (Mala Vaggo). In this chapter, there are twenty-three verses. These verses concern the "rust" that collects in one's life. These are the afflictions that take over our minds and manifest in unwholesome actions such as anger. The verses show you the path in order to get rid of these impurities from your life.

The chapter dedicated to the Dhamma (Dhammattha Vaggo) is the nineteenth chapter. In this chapter, there are seventeen verses about the life that is well established on the teachings of the Buddha.

The Noble Eightfold Path is the only way that leads to the freedom of suffering, Nibbāna. The chapter entitled the Path (Magga Vaggo) elaborates the way to Nibbāna through seventeen verses.

The twenty-first chapter is on the Miscellaneous (Pakinnaka Vaggo). This contains collections of teachings on different topics. There are sixteen verses. These verses show the path to a sorrow-free life.

The ungrateful person is most likely destined to be reborn in hell. Fearing rebirth in hell, one should fully abandon evil and unrighteous qualities. The fourteen verses in the twenty-second chapter on Hell (Niraya Vaggo) remind us of the danger we should avoid.

"Nāga" in Pāli language is a term for the elephant. Chapter twenty-three is about the Elephant (Nāga Vagga). The Buddha utters fourteen verses using the simile of an elephant.

The second Noble Truth taught by the Buddha is the Noble Truth of the cause of suffering. The cause for the suffering of the cycle of rebirth is craving. The cause of suffering must be fully eradicated. In the chapter on Craving (Tanhā Vaggo), you can learn twenty-six verses about the true nature of craving.

Preface

The twenty-fifth chapter is on Enlightened Monks (Bhikkhu Vaggo). There are twenty-three verses. The perfection of the monk life is to become an enlightened monk by culminating the practice of virtue, concentration, and wisdom. These verses introduce the ideal monk life to the world.

The final chapter of the Dhammapada is on the True Brahmin (Brāhmana Vaggo). The Brahmin Clan was the most highly respected clan in the ordinary society in the time of the Buddha in India. However, the Buddha never describes that a person is noble and sacred merely through one's clan, wealth, power, or ordinary knowledge. Rather, Buddha describes that a person becomes noble and sacred through his noble qualities. Therefore, the Buddha uses the term "Brahmin" to describe the enlightened monk. You can read forty-one verses about the true Brahmin in this chapter.

There are four hundred and twenty-three eloquent verses in this book titled "What Does the Buddha Really Teach?—Dhammapada". May you have a wonderful opportunity to learn the meanings of these sacred verses and practice the awakening teachings diligently in your life! May you experience the peace of true freedom!

May all the monks and lay people who contributed the development of this book attain the peace of true freedom! May you who is reading this sacred book with much respect, also attain the peace of true freedom!

With loving kindness,

Kiribathgoda Ñānānanda Thera.

Mahamevnawa Monestery

Waduwawa, Yatigaloluwa, Plogawela.

Sri Lanka

August 2016

1. PAIRS

1. All actions in this life are preceded by mind. Mind is their chief. They are made by mind. If one speaks or acts with an impure mind, suffering follows one like the wagon wheel that follows the foot of the ox.

2. All actions in this life are preceded by mind. Mind is their chief. They are made by mind. If one speaks or acts with a pure mind, happiness follows one like one's never-departing shadow.

3. "He abused me, he attacked me, he defeated me, and he robbed me." Those who harbour such thoughts will never end their hatred.

4. "He abused me, he attacked me, he defeated me, and he robbed me." Those who do not harbour such thoughts will end their hatred.

5. Hatred never ends through hatred; by non-hatred alone does it end. This is an eternal law in this world.

6. The people who quarrel do not realize that one day through these quarrels they will die, but those who do realize this fact settle their quarrels.

7. Whoever lives focused on pleasant things, with their sense faculties unguarded, immoderate in eating, lazy and sluggish, will be overpowered by Māra, just as a storm throws down a weak tree.

8. Whoever lives focused on the unpleasant nature of things, with their sense faculties guarded, moderate in eating, faithful and diligent, will not be overpowered by Māra, just as a storm cannot shake a rocky mountain.

9. Whoever is defiled, devoid of self-control and truthfulness and yet wears the monk's robe is surely not worthy of the robe.

10. Whoever has removed defilements, is well established in virtue, and is filled with self-control and truthfulness is indeed worthy of the robe.

11. In this world, there are unbeneficial things. Some people mistake these unbeneficial things to be beneficial. They also mistake the beneficial things, such as developing virtue, concentration, and wisdom, to be unbeneficial. They are enveloped in wrong thoughts. They never reach what is beneficial.

What Does the Buddha Really Teach?

12. Based on right view, some people always think right thoughts. These wise people know the beneficial things, such as developing virtue, concentration, and wisdom, to be beneficial. They also know the unbeneficial things to be unbeneficial. That is why they reach the most beneficial, Nibbāna.

13. Just as rain breaks through a poorly roofed house, lust penetrates the mind that has not been developed by calming and insight meditations.

14. Just as rain does not break through a well roofed house, lust never penetrates the mind that has been well developed by calming and insight meditations.

15. The evil-doer grieves in this life and in the next. He grieves in both worlds. He laments and is afflicted, seeing his own defiled actions.

16. The maker of merit rejoices in this life and in the next. He rejoices in both worlds. He rejoices and is delighted, seeing his own pure actions.

17. The evil-doer feels regret in this life and in the next. He feels regret in both worlds. He is

regretful knowing, "I have done evil." He is more regretful once he is reborn in the plane of misery.

18. The maker of merits is delighted in this life and in the next. He is delighted in both worlds. He is delighted in knowing, "I have made merit." He is delighted even more once he is reborn in heaven.

19. Even though the negligent person preaches much Dhamma to others, he does not practice accordingly. He is like a cowherd who only counts the cows of others. He does not attain the stages of enlightenment as a monk.

20. Even if the person practicing Dhamma preaches little to others, he lives according to the Dhamma. With developed knowledge and a well-freed mind, he abandons passion, hatred, and delusion. Not clinging to anything in this world or the next, he attains the stages of enlightenment as a monk.

2. DILIGENCE

21. The one who develops virtue, concentration, and wisdom diligently reaches the deathless, Nibbāna. The negligent, one who is intoxicated by sense pleasures, repeatedly dies. The diligent Dhamma practitioner goes beyond death. The negligent are as if already dead.

22. The diligent, wise Dhamma practitioner clearly understands the difference between diligence and negligence. Delighting in the dwelling of the noble ones which is the thirty-seven aids to enlightenment, they rejoice in diligence.

23. Wise, energetic disciples of the Buddha meditate frequently. Working hard, they practice the Dhamma, giving it top priority. They experience the incomparable freedom from bondage, Nibbāna.

24. The wise person is energetic, mindful, pure in conduct, considerate in action, self-restrained, and righteous. That diligent person's glory grows day by day.

25. The wise disciple of the Buddha practices the Dhamma energetically, diligently, with self-restraint, and with self-control. He makes

for himself the island called Nibbāna, which no flood can overwhelm.

26. Unwise, foolish people indulge in sense pleasures. They are caught up in negligence. But the wise protect diligence as their best treasure.

27. [Unwise, foolish people waste their life celebrating auspicious times.] Do not give yourself to negligence; do not become intoxicated with sense pleasures. Do not indulge in sense pleasures. If you meditate diligently you can attain great happiness.

28. The wise disciple of the Buddha drives away negligence with diligence. Ascending from the palace of wisdom, freed from sorrow, this sage looks at sorrowing people. It is like someone standing on a mountain observing those on the ground below.

29. The wise sage is diligent among the negligent. He is awake and meditates when others sleep. He advances like a swift horse leaving the weak one behind.

30. Sakka, the leader of gods, collected lots of merit diligently when he was in the human world as the youth Magha. That is how he

became the greatest of the gods. Diligence is always praised by Buddhas, and negligence is always despised.

31. The monk who delights in diligence and fears negligence reaches Nibbāna, destroying all bonds, large and small, like a fire burning everything in its path.

32. The monk who delights in diligence and fears negligence is incapable of losing wholesome qualities. He is close to Nibbāna.

3. THE MIND

33. The mind is so fickle and agitated. It is very difficult to protect and very challenging to guard from evil. The wise person straightens his mind as an arrow maker straightens an arrow shaft.

34. Like a fish that is pulled out of the water and thrown on the dry ground thrashes about and quivers, the mind thrashes about from thought to thought. That is why one should try to escape from the realm of Māra.

35. The mind is so difficult to subdue. It is unreliable. It seizes whatever it desires. Good indeed, it is to tame such a mind. A tamed mind brings happiness.

36. It is so difficult to detect the true nature of the mind. The mind is extremely subtle and seizes whatever it desires. A guarded mind brings happiness.

37. The mind dwells in the cave of the heart. It is without a body and wanders far and alone. Those who restrain this mind will be freed from Māra's bonds.

38. If one's mind is not firm in the Dhamma practice, if he does not know true Dhamma, and if his faith wavers, his wisdom never matures.

39. Because the mind of the energetic meditator is not soaked by lust, nor afflicted by hate—and because he has gone beyond both merit and demerit—there is no fear in him at all.

40. Realizing that this body is as fragile as a clay pot, guarding the mind like a well-guarded city, one should battle Māra with the sword of wisdom. Then, one should protect what has been won, and never find a resting place in this journey of rebirths.

41. This body indeed will not last long. Once the consciousness is released from the body, it will be cast aside and lie on the ground, like a useless log.

42. Whatever harm an enemy does to an enemy or a hater to a hater, a wrongly directed mind does greater harm to oneself.

43. Neither mother, nor father, nor any other relative can help one establish one's mind on the Dhamma. One becomes a great person due to one's well directed mind.

4. FLOWERS

44. Who will overcome this earth? Who will overcome this plane of misery? Who will overcome this world with its gods? Who will realize well taught words of Dhamma, as an expert garland maker selects beautiful flowers?

45. The trainee in the Dhamma path will overcome this earth. He will overcome the plane of misery. He will overcome this world with its gods. The trainee will realize the well taught words of Dhamma, as an expert garland maker selects beautiful flowers.

46. Understanding that this body is fragile like foam, realizing life's mirage-like nature, cutting off Māra's flowers of defilements, go beyond the sight of Māra!

47. The person obsessed by sense pleasures chases after them as a garland maker searches for flowers. Māra carries away that person to the plane of misery like a great flood sweeps away a sleeping village.

48. The person obsessed by sense pleasures chases after them as a garland maker searches for flowers. Although he has not fully satisfied

himself with sense pleasures, Māra brings him under his control.

49. As a bee gathers nectar from the flower and flies away without harming the flower's beauty or its fragrance, just so the sage goes on his alms round in the village.

50. Do not consider what is false in what others say or what they have or have not done. Consider instead what you have or have not done.

51. A beautiful flower that is colourful but without fragrance is not perfect. In the same way, the well spoken words of the Buddha become fruitless for the person who does not practice them.

52. A beautiful flower that is colourful and also fragrant is perfect. In the same way, well spoken words of the Buddha become fruitful for the person who practices them.

53. As an expert garland maker makes many garlands from a heap of flowers, you who obtained the human life should do many wholesome deeds.

54. The scent of flowers does not go against the wind. The scent of sandalwood, jasmine,

and rosebay does not go against the wind. But the scent of a grateful person does travel against the wind. The scent of his virtues spreads in all directions.

55. Of all the fragrances—sandalwood, rosebay, water lily, and jasmine—the fragrance of virtue is the sweetest.

56. Slight is the scent of rosebay or sandalwood, but the scent of the virtuous is supreme, drifting even to heaven.

57. The liberated ones are virtuous and practice the Dhamma diligently. They are freed from suffering by the realization of the Noble Truths. Māra never finds the path by which they are liberated.

58. In the roadside ditch, in a heap of rubbish, blooms a lotus, sweet smelling and pleasing to the eyes.

59. In the same way, among the rubbish heap of unaware ordinary people, the disciple of the Supreme Buddha shines brightly with wisdom.

5. THE FOOL

60. Night is long for one lying awake. Seven miles is long for one exhausted. The journey of rebirth is long for fools who do not realize the true Dhamma.

61. You should find a friend who has better qualities than you or has equal qualities. If you do not find such a friend, with great determination, you should live alone. There is no friendship with fools.

62. The fool is occupied with worldly things saying, "I have children! I have wealth!" In reality, one's self is not even one's own. How then are children? How then is wealth?

63. The fool who knows his foolishness is wise to that extent. But a fool who considers himself wise is the one indeed to be called a fool.

64. Though a fool associates with a wise person for his entire life, he never understands the Dhamma like the spoon that never tastes the flavour of soup.

65. Though a wise person associates with a wise person only for a moment, he quickly real-

izes this Dhamma, like the tongue that tastes the flavour of the soup.

66. Fools with no wisdom act as their own enemies. They live doing much evil. Eventually, their evil deeds will bear bitter fruit.

67. No deed is good that one regrets having done. No deed is good if the result is to be experienced with weeping and a tear-streaked face.

68. A deed is good when one does not regret having done it. A deed is good if the result is to be experienced with joy and delight.

69. As long as the results of evil deeds have not ripened, the fool thinks doing evil is as sweet as honey. But when the evil deeds ripen, then the fool suffers greatly.

70. The foolish ascetic who eats food with the tip of a blade of grass, month after month, is not worth a sixtieth part of the lives of the liberated ones who have realized the Dhamma.

71. It is true that fresh milk curdles immediately, but the result of one's evil deed does not ripen immediately. Rather, smoldering like fire covered by ashes, the result of the evil deed follows the fool looking for a chance to ripen.

72. The knowledge gained by the fool leads to his own ruin. He destroys his remaining goodness entirely. Finally, he cuts off his own head, namely his own wisdom.

73. The foolish monk always desires to gain honour from others. He seeks leadership over fellow monks. He is greedy for authority in the monasteries. He desires gifts and homage from householders.

74. The foolish monk thinks, "both householders and monks must seek advice only from me. In every task, they must follow my instructions." These intentions only increase his evil wishes and pride.

75. The way to worldly gain, honour, fame, and praise is one thing. The way to Nibbāna is another. The monk, the disciple of the Buddha, clearly understands this distinction. Therefore, he does not delight in honour. His top priority is living in seclusion.

6. THE WISE

76. When the wise person sees your faults, he points them out and helps you to improve. It is as if he guides you to a hidden treasure. Associate with such a wise person. As a result, only good will come, not bad.

77. A noble friend advises you, instructs you, and restrains you from doing evil. Such a noble friend is pleasing to grateful people but displeasing to the ungrateful.

78. Do not associate with evil friends. Do not associate with people with evil intentions. Associate with noble friends. Associate with the best of people who are full of wholesome qualities.

79. The wise person tranquilises his mind through the realization of Dhamma. He lives happily rejoicing in the Dhamma. He always delights in the true Dhamma taught by the noble ones.

80. Irrigators guide water to wherever it is needed. Arrow makers shape arrows to fit to task. Carpenters fashion wood for the desired design. The wise tame themselves in the same way.

81. As a solid mass of rock is not shaken by a storm, so too the wise are not moved by praise or blame.

82. As a deep lake that is clear and still, so too are the wise, having listened to the true Dhamma.

83. Noble people let go of desire for everything. They do not speak deceptively in order to gain pleasures and desires. Touched by happiness or unhappiness, the wise show no elation or depression.

84. The wise person neither commits evil for his own sake nor for the sake of others. He neither desires children, nor wealth, nor kingdom unfaithfully. He does not desire any success by unrighteous means. He is indeed virtuous, wise, and righteous.

85. Few, among humans, cross over the journey of rebirth to the farther shore called Nibbāna. The rest, the majority of people, only run about on this shore.

86. Those who act according to the perfectly taught Dhamma will reach Nibbāna, by crossing the realm of Māra, which is difficult to cross.

87. The wise person abandons unwholesome things and cultivates wholesome things. Then, abandoning household life, that person becomes a monk or a nun and enters the solitude, which is hardly enjoyed by ordinary people.

88. The wise person seeks delight in solitude, abandoning sense pleasures. Heading towards ultimate purification, he cleanses himself of the things that defile the mind.

89. Liberated ones' minds have reached full maturity in the enlightenment factors. Giving up all grasping, they delight in Nibbāna. Since they have destroyed impurities, they glow with wisdom. They are the ones who attain ultimate freedom in this world.

7. THE LIBERATED ONE

90. The liberated one has reached the end of the journey of rebirths. He is freed of sorrow. He is liberated in all ways. He is released from all bonds; therefore, no fever of passion exists in him.

91. The liberated ones are well established in mindfulness. They are always focused on the purity of their mind. They are not attached to anything. Like swans flying from a lake, they abandon their dwelling places time after time and leave unattached.

92. The liberated ones do not store up material items. They have understood the real nature of the food they consume. Their minds are focused on the meditative objects of emptiness, signlessness, and Nibbāna. Their path cannot be traced, like that of birds in the sky.

93. The liberated ones have destroyed all impurities. They are unattached to food. Their minds are focused on the meditative objects of emptiness, signlessness, and Nibbāna. Their steps cannot be traced, like that of birds in the sky.

94. The liberated ones' sense faculties are greatly subdued like horses well trained by a charioteer. They have abandoned conceit and are without impurities. Even the gods cherish such liberated ones who have unshaken minds.

95. The liberated one does not offend anyone. He is not shaken by ups and downs like the great earth. He is firm in virtue like a deep established stone pillar. He is like a lake without mud. For such liberated ones, there is no more wandering in the journey of rebirths.

96. The liberated one is calm in mind, calm in speech, and calm in action. He is liberated through right understanding. Such a person is fully at peace.

97. If someone has gone beyond faith and obtained personal experience, is not grateful to the five groups of clinging, has severed the links of the dependent origination, has destroyed the potential for rebirth, and has thrown out all defilements, he truly is the most excellent of humans.

98. Whether in a village, forest, valley, or on a hill, wherever liberated ones dwell, delightful indeed, is that place.

99. Delightful are forests, where the sense pleasure-seekers do not delight. There, the liberated ones delight, for they seek no sense pleasures.

8. THE THOUSANDS

100. Better than a thousand unbeneficial words is one beneficial word which, having been heard, brings peace.

101. Better than a thousand unbeneficial verses is one beneficial line of verse which, having been heard, brings peace.

102. Better than reciting a hundred unbeneficial verses is one line of Dhamma which, having been heard, brings peace.

103. Greater than a person who conquers a thousand people in battle a thousand times is the person who conquers himself in the battle of defilements.

104. Certainly it is better to conquer oneself than others. The person who tames himself and always restrains sense faculties wins the battle.

105. Neither a god, nor a divine musician, nor Māra, nor brahma, can turn into defeat the victory of a person who has conquered himself.

106. Better than a thousand ritual sacrifices offered every month for a hundred years is one

moment's gift offered to a liberated one who has fully developed his mind.

107. Better than a hundred years in the forest tending a ritual fire is one moment's gift offered to a liberated one who has fully developed his mind.

108. Whatever gift or offering a merit-seeker might perform in an entire year is not worth one-fourth as much as worshiping the liberated ones.

109. For the person who worships virtuous people and always reveres and serves the elders, four things increase: long life, beauty, happiness, and power.

110. Better it is to live one day virtuous and meditative than to live a hundred years devoid of virtue and stillness of mind.

111. Better it is to live one day wise and meditative than to live a hundred years devoid of wisdom and stillness of mind.

112. Better it is to live one day energetic and resolute than to live a hundred years lazy and sluggish.

113. Better it is to live one day seeing the arising and passing of five groups of clinging than to live a hundred years without ever seeing their arising and passing.

114. Better it is to live one day experiencing Nibbāna than to live a hundred years without ever experiencing Nibbāna.

115. Better it is to live one day realizing the Supreme Dhamma than to live a hundred years without ever realizing the Supreme Dhamma.

9. EVIL

116. Be quick to do meritorious deeds involving generosity, virtue, and meditation! Restrain your mind from evil! When one is slow to make merit one's mind delights in evil.

117. Having done something evil, do not repeat it; do not wish to do it again. Suffering is another name for evil.

118. Having done something meritorious, repeat it, wish for it. Happiness is another name for merit.

119. Evil deeds seem to be sweet for the evil doer as long as the evil has yet to ripen. But when the evil ripens, the evil doer sees the painful results of his evil deeds.

120. Meritorious deeds seem to be bitter as long as they have yet to ripen. But when the meritorious deeds ripen, the merit-maker will see the pleasant results of his meritorious deeds.

121. Do not think lightly of evil, saying, "It will not come back to me!" Drop by drop is the water pot filled. Likewise, the fool gathering it little by little is filled with evil.

122. Do not think lightly of merit, saying, "It will not come back to me!" Drop by drop is the water pot filled. Likewise, the wise person gathering it little by little is filled with merit.

123. A merchant with great wealth but with few employees avoids dangerous routes. The person who loves life avoids poison. So should you avoid evil deeds.

124. A hand that has no wounds can carry any poison. Without a wound, poison does not enter into the body. In the same way, there are no evil consequences for one who does no evil.

125. Like fine dust thrown against the wind, the result of evil comes back to the fool who offends a harmless, pure, liberated one.

126. Some are reborn in a womb. Evil doers are reborn in hell. Merit-makers go to heaven. Those without impurities attain ultimate freedom at passing away.

127. You will not find a place in the world—not in the sky, not in the middle of the ocean, not inside a mountain cave—where you can escape from the results of your evil deeds.

128. You will not find a place in the world— not in the sky, not in the middle of the ocean, not inside a mountain cave— where death will not overtake you.

10. VIOLENCE

129. All beings tremble at violence. All beings fear death. Putting yourself in the place of another, do not kill or influence others to kill.

130. All beings tremble at violence. Life is dear to all. Putting yourself in the place of another, do not kill or influence others to kill.

131. If desiring happiness, one uses violence to harm beings who also desire happiness, one will not find happiness after death.

132. If desiring happiness, one does not use violence to harm beings who also desire happiness, one will find happiness after death.

133. Do not speak harshly to anyone. What you say will be said back to you. Aggressive speech is painful, and retaliation will overtake you.

134. If, like a silenced broken metal bowl, you restrain your speech and silence yourself, you have approached Nibbāna. Then no hostility will be found in you.

135. As a cowherd drives cows to a meadow with a stick, so does aging and death drive beings to the end of their life.

136. When the fool commits evil deeds, he does not realise their seriousness. Eventually those people lacking wisdom are scorched by the results of their own deeds, like someone burned by fire.

137-140. Whoever uses violence to harm the non-violent and compassionate liberated ones will soon face one of ten miseries: intense physical pain, disaster, bodily injury, insanity, serious illness, oppression from rulers, grave charges, loss of relatives, wealth destroyed, or houses consumed by fire. With the breakup of the body, the foolish one is reborn in hell.

141. No nakedness or matted hair, no stained teeth, no fasting, no lying on the ground, no smearing oneself with ashes and dust, no sitting on the heels as austerities can purify the life of an ordinary person who has not overcome doubt.

142. Even though he is well adorned, if he practices the Dhamma, is calm, is restrained in senses, is established well in the path of

Nibbāna, is celibate, and has given up violence towards all beings—he truly is a Brāhmin, an ascetic, a monk.

143. Rarely found is the person in this world who is restrained by shame of wrong doing. That person restrains himself by disliking blame as a thoroughbred horse avoids the whip disliking punishment.

144. The thoroughbred horse struck by the whip becomes more alert. In the same way, you also must become disenchanted with this journey of rebirths. With faith, virtue, effort, and stillness of mind you must practice the Dhamma diligently. You must make decisions only through insight. Your realization must match your conduct. With established mindfulness, destroy this great suffering.

145. Irrigators guide water to wherever it is needed. Arrow makers shape arrows to fit to task. Carpenters fashion wood for the desired design. In the same way, the obedient ones tame themselves.

11. OLD AGE

146. When this world is burning all over by the flames of passion, hate, delusion, aging, sickness, death, sorrow, lamentation, pain, grief, and despair, why this laughter? Why this joy? Surrounded by the darkness of ignorance, why do you not search for light?

147. Look at the true nature of this body! Though decorated beautifully, this body is a skeleton plastered by heaps of flesh. It is a series of illnesses. Though ignorant people consider it with much appreciation, in this body there is nothing stable or lasting.

148. This body is wearing out. This is like a nest of diseases and so fragile. Filth oozes from nine openings. Life ends in death.

149. These grey skulls are like dried gourds that lie scattered about in autumn. Upon seeing them, how can one seek delight in sense pleasures?

150. This body is like a city that is built of bones, plastered with flesh and blood. It is surely subject to aging and death. It is this same body

that becomes an object for conceit and ungratefulness.

151. Even gorgeous royal chariots wear out, and indeed this body too wears out. But the good qualities of noble people do not decay. Thus, calm sages teach this truth to the grateful people.

152. The person who lacks Dhamma knowledge grows old like a bull. He grows only in flesh, but his wisdom does not grow.

153. Through many births, in this journey of misery, I have wandered on and on, searching for the builder of this house of suffering. To be born again and again is indeed suffering!

154. Oh house-builder, you are seen! You will not build a house for me again. All the rafters are broken into pieces and the ridgepole is shattered. My mind has reached the unconditioned. I have attained the destruction of craving.

155. Those who, in their youth, have not lived the chaste life, practiced the Dhamma, or have failed to acquire wealth are staring off into empty space like old cranes in a pond without fish.

156. Foolish people, in their youth, do not live the chaste life, nor do they practice the spiritual path. They do not even acquire wealth. They lie sighing over the past like worn out arrows shot from a bow.

12. ONESELF

157. If one holds oneself dear, one should guard oneself with care. Avoiding evil, the wise person should watch over himself at least in one of these three stages of life—childhood, adulthood, or old age.

158. One should first establish oneself in good qualities; then only should one instruct others. Thus, the wise person will not be stained.

159. As one instructs others, so should one act; if one would tame others, one should first be well tamed. Truly, it is very hard to tame oneself.

160. Oneself, indeed, is one's own protector. Who else could the protector be? With oneself well tamed, one can obtain the protection of Dhamma which is hard to obtain.

161. The evil a foolish person does by himself, born of himself, and produced by himself, grinds him as the diamond which was produced by the gems grinds similar types of gems.

162. The plant vines with big leaves cover the sal tree on which it grows. As a result, eventually the tree breaks down. In the same way,

the person who completely covers himself with his own corrupt conduct does to himself what an enemy wishes for him.

163. Easy to do are things that are bad and harmful to oneself. However, it is very difficult to do things that are good and beneficial for oneself.

164. The fool, relying on evil views, scorns the teaching of the liberated ones who live righteously. The fool produces fruit that destroys himself, like the bamboo tree produces fruit bringing its own destruction.

165. Through one's own evil deeds one is defiled. By avoiding evil deeds one is purified. Purity or impurity entirely depends on oneself; no one can purify another.

166. Do not lose your own welfare for the sake of others' welfare. Clearly understand your own welfare which is the attainment of enlightenment. Therefore, work hard to be a liberated one.

13. THE WORLD

167. Do not chase after sense pleasures; they are inferior in the world. Do not live with negligence. Do not follow a wrong view. Do not prolong the journey of rebirths.

168. Do not be negligent! Rouse yourself! Practice the Dhamma, living a life of good conduct. The Dhamma practitioner lives happily, both in this world and the next.

169. Practice the Dhamma, living a life of good conduct. Do not live a life of bad conduct. The Dhamma practitioner lives happily, both in this world and the next.

170. If one sees the world as a water bubble that is subject to destruction, and as a mirage that will soon disappear, one will not be seen by Māra.

171. Come, look at the true nature of this world, which is like a decorated royal chariot. Fools flounder in this world, but the wise have no attachment to this world.

172. Whoever was negligent before but later does no evil illuminates this world like the moon freed from clouds.

173. Whoever covers the evil he has done with wholesome deeds illuminates this world like the moon freed from clouds.

174. All beings in this world are blinded by the darkness of ignorance. Only a few see the true nature. As only a few birds escape from the net of the bird hunter, few beings go to heaven.

175. Swans fly in the sky. Liberated ones with psychic powers travel through the air. Having conquered Māra and his army, those wise sages are led away from the world.

176. A liar who violates the one law of truthfulness, rejects the existence after death. Therefore, there is no evil that he cannot do.

177. Truly, misers never go to heaven. Fools, indeed, never praise generosity. But the wise rejoice in generosity, and so find happiness hereafter.

178. Better than sole dominance over the earth, going to heaven, or lordship over all the worlds is the fruit of stream entry.

14. THE BUDDHA

179. The Buddha's victory over defilements cannot be undone. Nothing in the world follows him to challenge it. The Buddha's field of knowledge is limitless. Defilement-free is his path. By what track can you trace such a trackless Buddha?

180. Craving is like a net; it wraps beings up in existence. That craving no longer exists in the Buddha. Therefore, there is no way that one can tempt the Buddha towards existence. The Buddha's field of knowledge is limitless. Defilement-free is his path. By what track can you trace such a trackless Buddha?

181. The Buddhas are wise and devoted to meditation and delight in the peace of renunciation. Such mindful ones, The Buddhas, even the gods hold dear.

182. It is difficult to be born as human. Difficult is the life of beings. It is difficult to gain the opportunity to hear the true Dhamma. Rare is the appearance of Buddhas.

183. To avoid all evil, to cultivate wholesome qualities, and to cleanse one's mind—this is the teaching of the Buddhas.

184. Patience is the highest virtue. The Buddhas say that Nibbāna is supreme. One who destroys others is no monk; one who harms others is no monk.

185. Not disparaging others, not destroying lives, practicing restraint by the monastic rules, moderation in food, dwelling in far away secluded forest monasteries, and devotion to meditation—this is the teaching of the Buddhas.

186. Not even with a shower of gold coins would a person find satisfaction in sense pleasures. They only give little gratification but much suffering. The wise person understands this reality.

187. The disciple of the fully enlightened Buddha finds no delight even in heavenly pleasures. He delights in the destruction of craving, Nibbāna.

188. People threatened by fear go to many refuges: to mountains, forests, parks, trees, and shrines.

189. Going for refuge to mountains, forest, parks, trees, and shrines is never a secure refuge; none of these is a supreme refuge. By going to such a refuge, one is not released from all suffering.

190. If one has gone for refuge to the Buddha, the teaching of the Buddha, and the disciples of the Buddha, he will realize with developed wisdom the Four Noble Truths.

191. The Four Noble Truths are suffering, the arising of suffering, the overcoming of suffering, and the Eightfold Path leading to the ending of suffering.

192. Going for refuge to the Buddha, the teachings of the Buddha, and the disciples of the Buddha is the secure refuge; this is the supreme refuge. By going to this refuge, one is released from all suffering.

193. The birth of the best of men, the Buddha is very rare; such a person is not born everywhere. Where such a wise hero is born, that entire clan flourishes in happiness.

194. To see the Buddhas is happiness. The hearing of the true Dhamma is happiness. The

harmony of the disciples of the Buddha is happiness. The diligent Dhamma practice of those in harmony is happiness.

195-196. He who offers gifts to those worthy of offerings, the Buddha or his disciples who have transcended obsessive thinking, passed beyond sorrow and lamentation. The merit of those who venerate such peaceful and fearless ones can never be calculated by any measure.

15. HAPPINESS

197. Ah, so happily we live, without hate among those with hate. Among people who hate, we live without hate.

198. Ah, so happily we live, without affliction among those afflicted by defilements. Among afflicted people, we live without affliction.

199. Ah, so happily we live, without agitation among those agitated by the pursuit of sense pleasures. Among people who are agitated, we live without agitation.

200. Ah, so happily we live, we who have no defilements. We shall feast on joy, as do the gods in the Ābhassara brahma world.

201. Victory gives rise to hate; the defeated dwell in pain. Giving up both victory and defeat, the sage dwells happily.

202. There is no fire like lust, no crime like hate, no suffering like the five groups of clinging, and no happiness higher than Nibbāna.

203. Hunger is the worst illness; conditioned things the worst suffering. For one who knows

this as it really is, Nibbāna is the foremost happiness.

204. Good health is the most precious gain; and happiness born from realisation of the truth is the greatest wealth. Trust is the greatest relative; Nibbāna the highest happiness.

205. By tasting the flavour of solitude and drinking the flavour of the excellent peace, Nibbāna, the monk becomes free of distress and evil.

206. It is good to see the noble ones; their company is always a delight. Free from the sight of fools, beings will always be happy.

207. One who keeps company with fools will be sad for a long, long time. Living with fools is painful, as is living with enemies. Living with the wise is delightful, like relatives gathered together.

208. Therefore, follow the noble ones, who are energetic, wise, knowledgeable, committed to virtue, and dutiful. One should follow such a grateful person who is truly wise, as the moon always dwells in the sky.

16. THE DEAR

209. Some people practice what they should not; they do not practice the greatest thing, the Dhamma. Clinging to what is dear, they abandon what is beneficial, but later they envy those who have succeeded in Dhamma practice.

210. Do not get too attached, even to your loved ones. Have no fellowship with disagreeable people. Not seeing your loved ones is suffering; seeing the disagreeable is also suffering.

211. Therefore, hold nothing dear, for separation from all that is dear is painful. There are no bonds for those who have nothing agreeable or disagreeable.

212. Longing gives rise to sorrow; longing gives rise to fear. For someone released from longing, there is no sorrow; so, from what would fear arise?

213. Affection gives rise to sorrow; affection gives rise to fear. For someone released from affection, there is no sorrow; so, from what would fear arise?

214. Desire gives rise to sorrow; desire gives rise to fear. For someone released from desire,

there is no sorrow; so, from what would fear arise?

215. Sense desire gives rise to sorrow; sense desire gives rise to fear. For someone released from sense desire, there is no sorrow; so, from what would fear arise?

216. Craving gives rise to sorrow; craving gives rise to fear. For someone released from craving, there is no sorrow; so, from what would fear arise?

217. If someone is virtuous, has insight into the Four Noble Truths, is established in the Dhamma, is truthful, and is endowed with righteous living—people hold that person dear.

218. The person who aspires to Nibbāna, though he does not reveal his goal to anyone, experiences Nibbāna in his mind. He is not bound by sense pleasures. Such a person is called "one bound up stream."

219-220. Relatives, friends, and companions welcome a long-absent person returning from abroad. Likewise, in passing from this world to the next, the merit one has collected welcomes him.

17. ANGER

221. Give up anger, give up conceit, and overcome all bonds of existence. There is no suffering for an enlightened one who does not cling to mentality and materiality.

222. The one who keeps anger in check as it arises, as a charioteer controls a speeding chariot, him I call a true charioteer. Others are merely rein-holders.

223. Conquer anger with non-anger, conquer wickedness with goodness, conquer stinginess with giving and conquer a liar with truth.

224. Speak the truth; do not get angry; and when asked, give even if you have only a little. By these three actions one can reach the presence of the gods.

225. The sages are harmless, they are ever restrained in body, and they go to the deathless state, Nibbāna, where having gone, they do not sorrow.

226. Those who practice the Dhamma constantly day and night, devoted to meditation,

and are always focused on Nibbāna—their impurities fade away.

227. Ancient is this situation, oh Atula, it is not just true today: people criticize one sitting silently, they criticize one speaking much, and they criticize one speaking moderately. There is no one in the world who is not criticized.

228. No person can be found who has been, is, or will be only criticized or only praised.

229. When a wise person praises somebody, he does so after carefully observing that person's flawless character, wisdom, virtue, and stillness of mind.

230. Who can criticize one who is as worthy as a coin made of the finest gold? Such a person is praised even by the gods, even by Brahma.

231. Guard against anger erupting in your body; be restrained with your body. Abandoning bodily misconduct, practice good conduct with your body.

232. Guard against anger erupting in your speech; be restrained with your speech. Abandoning verbal misconduct, practice good conduct with your speech.

233. Guard against anger erupting in your mind; be restrained with your mind. Abandoning mental misconduct, practice good conduct with your mind.

234. The wise are restrained in body, restrained in speech, and restrained in mind. They are fully restrained.

18. STAIN

235. Your life is now like a yellowed, withered leaf. The wardens of hell are standing by. You have reached death's door of downfall. Yet, it seems that you have made no merit as provision for your journey!

236. Make an island for yourself. Be quick in making effort and become a wise person. Remove the stain of defilements and become undefiled. Enter the divine realm of the noble ones.

237. You are now at the end of your life. You are headed to the presence of the King of Hell. You have not got much time to live. Yet it seems that you have made no merit as provision for your journey!

238. Make an island for yourself. Be quick in making effort and become a wise person. Remove stain of defilements and become undefiled. You must not come back again to this world of birth and decay.

239. The wise person, gradually, bit by bit, moment by moment, must cleanse his mind of

the stain of defilements as a gold smith cleanses gold by removing stains.

240. As rust born from iron eats away the very iron that formed it, so does the reckless behaviour of a monk lead him to the plain of misery.

241. Oral teachings become stained when not recited frequently, homes become stained by inactivity, laziness stains physical beauty, and negligence stains the guardian.

242. Misbehaviour is a stain in a woman. Stinginess is a stain in a giver. Stains, indeed, are all evil things, both in this world and the next.

243. Ignorance is the greatest stain among all stains. Having removed this stain, monks become stainless!

244. Easy is life for someone without shame of wrongdoing, who is bold as a crow, ungrateful, arrogant, and corrupt.

245. Difficult is life for someone who has shame of wrongdoing, who is always searching for purity, innocent, cautious, and values righteous living.

246-247. One who kills beings, lies, steals, goes to another man's wife, and drinks intoxicants—such a man digs up his own grave here in this world.

248. Good man, know this: evil destroys one's restraint. Do not let greed and wickedness drag you to the plain of misery, where you will suffer for a long time.

249. People give according to their faith and confident mind. This being the case, if one becomes discontented with the food and drink given by others, one cannot attain stillness of mind, either by day or by night.

250. But if one discards this discontent by cutting it out and uprooting it, one can attain stillness of mind, both by day and by night.

251. There is no fire like lust, no trap like hate, no net like delusion, and no river like craving.

252. It is easy to see the fault of others, but hard to see one's own. One sifts out the faults of others like chaff but conceals one's own as a crafty bird-hunter hides behind camouflage.

253. If one focuses on other's faults and constantly takes offense, one's own impurities increase and one is far from the destruction of impurities.

254. Birds do not leave tracks in the sky. No monk exists outside the Buddha's path. People delight in obsessive thoughts, but the Buddhas are free of obsessive thinking.

255. Birds do not leave tracks in the sky. No monk exists outside the Buddha's path. No conditioned things are eternal. No agitation exists for Buddhas.

19. ON DHAMMA

256. If a judge rules unfairly in a case he is not just. The wise person makes decisions by properly investigating both right and wrong.

257. He who does not judge a case unfairly, that wise person is protected by the Dhamma. He is called the one who is established in the Dhamma.

258. One is not wise only because one speaks a lot. If one does not cause fear in others, is devoid of hate, and is fearless, one can truly be called a wise person.

259. One is not an upholder of the Dhamma only because he preaches a lot. Having heard even a little, if one experiences the Dhamma personally and is never negligent of the Dhamma practice, one is indeed an upholder of the Dhamma.

260. Grey hair does not make a monk an elder. Someone ripe only in age is called "an old fool".

261. If there is truthfulness, Dhamma, harmlessness, restraint, and self-control in a monk

and if that wise monk has purged himself of defilements, that monk is called an elder.

262. Not through sweet voice or by good looks alone can one become a person of good character. If one is jealous, selfish, and deceitful, one does not become a person of good character.

263. But with bad qualities cut off, uprooted, and destroyed, one who is wise and has purged himself of bad qualities is called one of good character.

264. Not by shaven head does one become a monk. If one is devoid of virtue, untruthful, and filled with evil desires and greed, how could such a person be a monk?

265. One who has, in every way, subdued all evil, small and great is, for that reason, called a monk.

266. One is not a monk just because one lives on others' alms. Nor does one become a monk by taking on evil ways.

267. Whoever in the Buddha's path sets aside both merit and demerit, lives the chaste life, and

goes through the world with true knowledge is called a monk.

268. Not by observing silence does an ignorant fool become a sage. The wise person selects what is good and avoids what is evil as if holding a balance-scale.

269. Whoever avoids evil, weighs the internal world and the external world with wisdom is, for that reason, called a sage.

270. Though people call one noble, one who harms beings is not noble. One is called noble because one is harmless to all beings.

271. Though you are dutiful, virtuous, knowledgeable in the Dhamma, have attained stillness of the mind, and live in far-away forest monasteries, you should not think, through overestimation that you have completed the path.

272. Oh monk, there is this bliss of renunciation not experienced by the ordinary people. You also should think, "I will attain that bliss". Do not trust this existence until you have attained liberation.

20. THE PATH

273. Of all paths, the Noble Eight Fold Path is the best. Of all truths, the Four Noble Truth is the best. Of all things, the passionless state, Nibbāna, is the best. Of all humans, the one with eyes of the Dhamma, Buddha, is the best.

274. This is the only path for purifying one's vision of truth; there is no other. Follow it and you will bewilder Māra.

275. By following the Noble Eight Fold Path you can put an end to suffering. I have taught you this path which pulls out arrows of defilements.

276. You, yourself, must make a strong effort to attain Nibbāna. Buddhas only point the way. Those who follow the path and those who meditate will be freed from Māra's bonds.

277. "All conditioned things are impermanent"—when one sees this with wisdom, one gives up admiration for suffering which is disguised as happiness. This is the path to purification, Nibbāna.

278. "All conditioned things are suffering"— when one sees this with wisdom, one gives

up admiration for suffering which is disguised as happiness. This is the path to purification, Nibbāna.

279. "All things are not-self"—when one sees this with wisdom, one gives up admiration for suffering which is disguised as happiness. This is the path to purification, Nibbāna.

280. The inactive one who does not exert himself when he should, who though young and strong is full of laziness, with a mind full of vain thoughts—such an indolent person does not find the path to wisdom.

281. Let a person be watchful in speech, well restrained in mind, and not commit evil by the body. Let him purify these three courses of action and fulfill the path taught by the sages.

282. Wisdom arises from calm and insight meditation. Without meditation wisdom decays. Knowing this two-way path for progress and decline, conduct yourself on the path which grows wisdom.

283. Oh monks, cut down the trees of defilements, but not the trees in the forest. From the trees of defilements, fear is born. Having cut

down both large and small trees of defilements be deforested of defilements.

284. As long as the underbrush of desire, even the slightest, of a man towards a woman is not cut down, his mind is in bondage, like the suckling calf to its mother.

285. Cut off craving as one plucks with his hand an autumn lotus. Cultivate only the path to excellent peace, Nibbāna, as taught by the Well Gone One, the Buddha.

286. "Here I will live in the rainy season, here in winter and summer"—thus thinks the fool. He does not realize the danger that death might intervene.

287. Some people live clinging to and intoxicated by children and wealth. Suddenly they are carried away to death by Māra, as a great flood carries away a sleeping village to the ocean.

288. For someone who is seized by Māra, there is no protection by relatives. No one can save him—not sons, not father, and not relatives.

289. Realizing this truth, let the wise person restrain himself with virtue. Let him quickly clear the path to Nibbāna.

21. MISCELLANEOUS

290. One who expects greater happiness must be able to give up lesser happiness. The wise person looking for the greater, Nibbāna, renounces the lesser, sense pleasures.

291. Those who seek their own happiness by causing suffering for others are entangled with hate. They will never be free from hate.

292. If someone rejects the Dhamma practice and does, instead, what they should not, impurities increase for that conceited and negligent person.

293. If someone's mind is constantly well established with mindfulness of the body and does not do what he should not do, impurities are destroyed for that mindful person with full awareness.

294. Having killed with wisdom, the mother called craving, the father called arrogance, the two warrior kings called eternalism and nihilism; and having destroyed the country called the internal and external sense bases, together with its treasurer called desire, the Brāhmin, free of suffering, goes to Nibbāna.

295. Having killed, with wisdom, the mother called craving, the father called arrogance, the two Brāhmin kings called eternalism and nihilism, the tiger called the five hindrances, the Brāhmin—free of suffering—goes to Nibbāna.

296. Those disciples of Gotama Buddha, who day and night constantly practice the meditation on the qualities of the Buddha, wake up happily every day.

297. Those disciples of Gotama Buddha, who day and night constantly practice the meditation on the qualities of the Dhamma, wake up happily every day.

298. Those disciples of Gotama Buddha, who day and night constantly practice the meditation on the qualities of the community of noble monks, wake up happily every day.

299. Those disciples of Gotama Buddha, who day and night constantly practice mindfulness of the body, wake up happily every day.

300. Those disciples of Gotama Buddha, whose minds by day and night delight in harmlessness, wake up happily every day.

301. Those disciples of Gotama Buddha, whose minds by day and night delight in calm and insight meditation, wake up happily every day.

302. Becoming a monk is difficult—it is hard to enjoy the monk life. Household life is also difficult—it is painful. Living with people who have different opinions is suffering. Wandering in the journey of rebirths is indeed suffering. Therefore, do not be a wanderer in saṁsāra; do not be a pursuer of suffering.

303. The lay disciple of the Buddha—endowed with faith, virtue, fame, and wealth—is respected wherever he goes.

304. Good people are seen from afar by the Buddha, like the Himalaya Mountain is visible from afar. But foolish people are unseen, even close up, like arrows shot in the night.

305. One should live alone, one should sleep alone, and having tamed oneself alone without being lazy, one should live in the forest, delighting there.

22. HELL

306. The liar who accuses a good person goes to hell; so does the one who, having done wrong, says, "I did not do it". Both these people of base actions become equal after death, by taking rebirth in hell.

307. There are many people wearing robes but with no restraint and with evil behaviours. These wicked people, because of their evil deeds, will be reborn in hell.

308. It is better to swallow flaming red-hot iron balls than to live as an immoral unrestrained monk and eat the alms-food of the people.

309. Four results come to the reckless man who engages in sexual misconduct with another's wife: accumulation of demerit, agitation, accusation, and rebirth in hell.

310. Evil is the rebirth of an evil-doer. Brief is the pleasure of the frightened man engaged with a frightened woman. If caught, the king will impose severe punishment. Therefore a man must not engage in sexual misconduct with another's wife.

311. Just as kusa grass cuts the hand that wrongly grasps it, so does the monk-life or the nun-life wrongly lived drag one to hell.

312. Virtue practised in a loose way, the defiled monk-life and nun-life, or a chaste life lived dubiously—none of these lead to much success in the Buddha's path.

313. If any good quality is to be practised, let one do it again with strong effort. A careless monk-life or nun-life stirs up even more defilements.

314. Evil deeds are better left undone—evil deeds torment the doer later. Good deeds are better done—for, having done them, the doer has no regret later.

315. Just as a border city is well guarded inside and out, so too guard yourself from evil— do not let slip this moment for spiritual practice. Those who let this moment pass will suffer after they have fallen into hell.

316. No need to be ashamed of wearing clothes, but the Niganthas are ashamed of wearing cloth. One should indeed be ashamed of nakedness, but the Niganthas are not ashamed

of nakedness. Those who take up wrong view take rebirth in the plane of misery.

317. No need to be afraid of Nibbāna, but the Niganthas are afraid of Nibbāna. One should indeed be afraid of holding wrong views. Those who take up wrong views take rebirth in the plane of misery.

318. Finding fault in the noble Dhamma and seeing no fault in wrong teachings, those who take up wrong views take rebirth in the plane of misery.

319. But knowing wrong teachings as wrong teachings and the noble Dhamma as noble Dhamma, those who take up right views take rebirth in the plane of bliss.

23. THE KING ELEPHANT

320. As a king elephant in battle endures arrows shot from bows all around, so I endure the verbal abuse of others. Indeed, many people in this world lack virtue.

321. The well-tamed elephant is the one whom people take into a crowd. The well-tamed elephant is the one even the king mounts. Best among humans is the tamed person who endures verbal abuse.

322. Excellent are well-tamed mules, thoroughbred Sindhu horses, tusker elephants and king elephants. But even more excellent is the person who has tamed himself.

323. Not by these vehicles, however, could one go to that place not gone to, Nibbāna, as one who is self-tamed goes by his own tamed and well-controlled mind.

324. During mating time, the tusker elephant named Dhanapāla was uncontrollable. Tied down, he did not even eat, but he spent his time remembering only the forest where his mother elephant lived. He waited to attend on

her needs showing her the quality of gratefulness.

325. If a person is sluggish and gluttonous, sleeps rolling around on a bed, he is like a fat, grain-fed pig. That fool comes to sleep in a womb again and again.

326. Formerly, this mind wandered about where it wished, as it liked, and as it pleased, but now, I will thoroughly master it with wisdom as an elephant keeper controls with his stick an elephant in its mating time.

327. Delight in diligence! Guard your mind well! Draw yourself out of this bog of defilements as an elephant that has sunken in mud draws himself out of the mud.

328. If you find an intelligent and grateful friend of good conduct, you should keep his company joyously and mindfully overcoming all dangers.

329. If you do not find an intelligent and grateful friend of good conduct, you should live alone like a king who leaves behind his conquered kingdom, or like the elephant Mātanga who left his herd and lived alone.

330. Better it is to live alone. There is no companionship with evil friends. Live alone, at ease, doing no evil like the king elephant Mātanga who left his herd and lived alone.

331. Happiness is having friends when need arises. Happiness is contentment with just what one has. Happiness is merit at the end of one's life. Happiness is the abandoning of all suffering.

332. In this world, serving one's mother is happiness, serving one's father is happiness, serving monks and nuns is happiness, and serving liberated ones is happiness.

333. Happiness is virtue until life's end; happiness is well established faith in the Buddha; happiness is the attainment of wisdom; and happiness is not doing evil.

24. CRAVING

334. The craving of a person who lives negligently spreads like a creeping vine. Like a monkey who leaps from tree to tree in the forest seeking fruits, that person leaps from life to life, in this journey of misery.

335. Whoever is overcome by this miserable, wretched, and sticky craving, his sorrow grows like rapidly growing grass after rain.

336. Whoever overcomes this miserable, wretched craving that is difficult to overcome, from him sorrow falls away like water drips from a lotus leaf.

337. This I say to you: Good luck to all assembled here! Dig up the root of craving like someone in search of the fragrant root of the bīrana grass. Do not let Māra crush you over and over again, as the flood crushes a bunch of bamboo trees on a bank of the river.

338. Just as a tree, though cut down, grows again if its roots are strong and remain uncut, so does suffering sprout again and again until the tendency of craving in the mind is rooted out.

339. Thirty-six streams of craving flow through pleasurable objects. The misguided person who is entangled by this craving is carried away to hell by the flood of lustful thoughts.

340. The stream of craving flows through every sense base and the creeper of craving sprouts and grows throughout your life. In seeing that the creeper has sprouted in you, cut off its roots with the sword of wisdom.

341. When craving flows through objects, feelings of pleasure arise in beings. They get attached to that pleasure and seek more enjoyment. Undoubtedly, these people are bound to the journey of birth and old age.

342. Surrounded by craving, these people run around frightened like a trapped rabbit. Held by fetters and bonds of defilements, they suffer repeatedly over a long time.

343. Surrounded by craving, these people run around frightened like a trapped rabbit. Therefore, the monk who wishes for passion-free Nibbāna should destroy his own craving.

344. There is a person who, turning away from the forest of defilements called household

life, delights in the monk life. But after being freed from the forest of defilements called the household life, he runs back to it. Look at that person! Though freed, he runs back to that very bondage!

345-346. If a person was bound with chains made of iron, shackles made of wood, and ropes made of hemp grass, those bonds are not called strong bonds by the wise. Instead, the infatuation and longing for jewels, ornaments, children and wives—that, they say, is a far stronger bond, which pulls one downwards all the way to hell, and, though seemingly loose, is hard to remove. This, too, the wise cut off. By abandoning sense pleasures, and without any longing, they become monks and nuns.

347. Those who are obsessed with passion and have fallen into the flood of craving, are like a spider, caught in its own web. This, too, the wise cut off. In order to abandon all suffering, without any longing for sense pleasures, wise people become monks and nuns.

348. Let go of regret over the past, let go of dreaming over the future, and let go of clinging to the present. Go beyond existence. With the

mind liberated in every way, do not come again and again to the world of birth and old age.

349. Some people are occupied with sensual thoughts. With a mind of strong lust, they focus on what is pleasant. In them, craving grows more and more. Indeed, they strengthen their bond of craving.

350. He who delights in subduing lustful thoughts, who meditates on the impurities of the body and is constantly mindful—it is he who will make an end of craving and will cut Māra's bond.

351. The monk who has reached the end goal, Nibbāna, is fearless, free from craving, free from defilements, and has plucked out the spikes called existence—for him, this is the last body.

352. The monk who is free from craving and attachment, is skilled in teaching the true meanings of the Dhamma, and knows the meaning of words and phrases,—he, indeed, is the bearer of his final body. He is truly called the profoundly wise one, the great man.

353. I have conquered all unwholesome things. I have realized everything. I am stained by nothing. Abandoning all, I am freed through the destruction of craving. Having thus, directly realized all by myself, whom shall I call my teacher?

354. The gift of Dhamma surpasses all gifts. The taste of Dhamma surpasses all taste. The delight in Dhamma surpasses all delights. The destruction of cravings conquers all suffering.

355. Wealth destroys those who lack in wisdom, but, those who seek Nibbāna are not destroyed like that. The foolish person is destroyed by his own craving for wealth, as if he had made someone destroy him.

356. Weeds are the ruin of fields; passion is the ruin of people. Therefore, what is offered to those free of passion bears great fruit.

357. Weeds are the ruin of fields; hatred is the ruin of people. Therefore, what is offered to those free of hatred bears great fruit.

358. Weeds are the ruin of fields; delusion is the ruin of people. Therefore, what is offered to those free of delusion bears great fruit.

359. Weeds are the ruin of fields; desire is the ruin of people. Therefore, what is offered to those free of desire bears great fruit.

25. THE MONK

360. Restraint of the eye is good. Good is restraint of the ear. Restraint of the nose is good. Good is restraint of the tongue.

361. Restraint of the body is good. Good is the restraint of speech. Restraint of the mind is good. Good is restraint in all circumstances. The monk who restrains in every way is freed from all suffering.

362. The one with hands restrained, feet restrained, speech restrained, who is foremost among the restrained, delights in inward stillness, keeps to himself, and is content; he is called a monk.

363. If a monk restrains his mouth, speaks insightfully, and is humble, he can illuminate the meanings and the Dhamma. Sweet is his speech.

364. The monk who dwells in the Dhamma, delights in the Dhamma, reflects on the Dhamma and recollects the Dhamma does not fall away from the true Dhamma.

365. A monk should not despise what he has received from donors, nor envy the gains of oth-

ers. The monk who envies the gains of others does not attain the stillness of mind.

366. A monk who does not despise what he has received from donors, even though it be little, who is pure in livelihood and energetic, is praised even by the gods.

367. He who has no notion of "mine" for mentality and materiality, who does not sorrow on the absence of them—he is truly called a monk.

368. The monk who dwells in loving-kindness and is deeply pleased with the Buddha's path attains the destruction of formations, Nibbāna.

369. Oh monk, from the boat of life, empty the water of inferior intentions! Emptied, it will sail lightly. Cutting off passion and hatred, you will quickly go to Nibbāna.

370. Cut off the five lower bonds, abandon the five higher bonds, and cultivate the five spiritual facilities. The monk who has overcome the five bonds called passion, hatred, delusion, conceits, and views is called "the one who has crossed the flood".

371. Oh monk, meditate! Do not be negligent! Do not let your mind whirl about in sense pleasures! Negligent, gone to hell, do not swallow red-hot iron balls, and then being burnt do not cry out, "Oh this is painful!"

372. There is no singleness of mind for one without wisdom. There is no wisdom for one without singleness of mind. He, who has both singleness of mind and wisdom, indeed, is close to Nibbāna.

373. The monk who has entered an empty hut and has calmed his mind, who contemplates the true nature of the five groups of clinging, in him there arises a delight that transcends all human delights.

374. Whenever one sees with insight the arising and passing of the five groups of clinging, he is full of joy and happiness. To the person who has realized the truth, this joy is the sweetest taste.

375. These three factors form the bases for a monk in contemplating the true nature of the five groups of clinging: guarding the senses, contentment, and restraint according to the monastic rules.

376. Associate with noble friends who live purely and energetically, be skillful in conduct and duties, and engage in Dhamma discussion. Thus, full of joy, make an end to this suffering.

377. Just as the jasmine creeper sheds its withered flowers, so, oh monk, shed passion and hatred from your mind!

378. The monk who is calm in body, calm in speech, peaceful, stilled in mind, and has rejected sense desire, he truly is called "the calm one."

379. By oneself one must censure oneself and investigate oneself. Oh monk, guarding yourself and establishing mindfulness, live at ease.

380. Oneself, indeed, is one's own protector. One does, indeed, make one's own destiny. Therefore, control yourself as the skilled merchant controls a fine horse.

381. Due to Dhamma practise, the monk who is filled with joy and pleased with the Buddha's path, attains peace, the destruction of formations, Nibbāna.

382. Even a young monk engaged in the Buddha's path illuminates this world like the moon freed from clouds.

26. THE TRUE BRĀHMIN

383. Oh Brāhmin, dry up this river of craving! Oh Brāhmin, dispel sense desire! Realizing the destruction of all the conditioned things, oh Brāhmin, become ungrateful to the five groups of clinging.

384. When the Brāhmin has reached the full culmination of calm and insight meditations, all bonds come to their end; realizing this truth, he becomes liberated.

385. He for whom there is neither this shore called internal sense bases nor the other shore called the external sense bases, nor both shores, and he who is released from defilements and free of distress, him do I call a true Brāhmin.

386. He who meditates, freed of the stain of defilements, who has completed the path to Nibbāna, is free from impurities, and has reached the highest goal, liberation, him do I call a true Brāhmin.

387. The sun shines by day, the moon glows at night. The warrior king shines in armour. A true Brāhmin shines in meditation. But all day and all night, the Buddha shines in splendour.

388. Because he has discarded evil, he is called a Brāhmin; because he is engaged in Dhamma and pure conduct, he is called a monk; and because he drives out his defilements, this person is called a monk.

389. One should not strike the liberated one, the true Brāhmin. He does not show anger, which no longer exists in him. Shame on the person who hits the true Brāhmin and a greater shame on the person who shows anger!

390. The quality of patience in a Brāhmin is not an insignificant quality. The hateful person enjoys hating. The liberated Brāhmin turns his mind away from thoughts of harming. To the extent the thoughts of harming wears away, to that extent does his suffering subside.

391. He who does no evil by body, speech, and mind, and is restrained in these three ways —him do I call a Brāhmin.

392. Just as a Brāhmin worships a fire ritual, so does the grateful person respectfully worship his teacher from whom he learnt the Dhamma that was taught by the fully enlightened Buddha.

393. Not by matted hair, nor by clan, and nor by birth does one become a Brāhmin. The one, who realizes the Four Noble Truths, follows Dhamma, and leads a pure life, is a true Brāhmin.

394. Oh one with little wisdom, what use is matted hair? What use is an antelope skin robe? Within you is the tangle of defilements; only outside do you groom.

395. The person who wears a robe made of discarded rags, who is lean, with veins showing all over the body, and who meditates alone in the forest—him do I call a Brāhmin.

396. I do not call him a Brāhmin because he was merely conceived into a Brāhmin mother's womb and was born from that Brāhmin mother. He is someone with defilements; therefore he is a venerable sir only by name. But he who is free from defilements and clinging—him do I call a Brāhmin.

397. He, who, has cut off all bonds, does not tremble at all, and, who has overcome all ties of defilements and is released from them—him do I call a Brāhmin.

398. He who has cut off the rope called hatred, the strong cord called craving, the great chain called wrong views, and he who has lifted up and destroyed the crossbar called ignorance and is enlightened—him do I call a Brāhmin.

399. He who endures abuse, beating, and punishment without hating and who has patience as his power and as his mighty army—him do I call a Brāhmin.

400. He who is free from anger, observant in proper conduct and duties, virtuous, without craving, self-controlled, and bears his final body—him do I call a Brāhmin.

401. Like a slipping water drop on a lotus leaf or a mustard seed falling off the point of a needle, he who is not attached to sense pleasures—him do I call a Brāhmin.

402. He who realizes for himself that his suffering will come to an end in this very life, who has laid aside the burden of defilements and is released from them—him do I call a Brāhmin.

403. He who has profound wisdom, who is extremely wise, skilled in distinguishing the

right path and wrong path, and has reached the highest goal, liberation—him do I call a Brāhmin.

404. He who does not mingle with householders, monks and nuns, is without craving, and is with few wishes—him do I call a Brāhmin.

405. He who has given up violence towards beings both fearless and fearful, who neither kills nor influences others to kill—him do I call a Brāhmin.

406. He who is friendly among those who oppose, is peaceful among the violent, and does not cling among those who cling—him do I call a Brāhmin.

407. He whose passion, hatred, conceit, and ungratefulness have fallen off from his mind like a mustard seed from the point of a needle—him do I call a Brahman.

408. He who speaks gentle, beneficial, sweet, and truthful words, who never makes others angry— him do I call a Brāhmin.

409. He who in this world does not steal anything, be it long or short, large or small, beautiful or not—him do I call a Brāhmin.

410. He who has no desire for this world or the next and who is desire-free and has been released from defilements—him do I call a Brāhmin.

411. He who has no craving, who through perfect realization is free from doubts, and has plunged into the deathless, Nibbāna—him do I call a Brāhmin.

412. He who has transcended ties of both merit and demerit here in this life, and is sorrowless, stainless, and pure—him do I call a Brāhmin.

413. He who, like the full moon, is spotless and pure, extremely serene and still, and has destroyed craving for existence—him do I call a Brāhmin.

414. He who has passed beyond the troublesome road of defilements, this difficult path, this journey of rebirths, this delusion; who has crossed over and reached the other shore; who is a meditator, free from craving, free from doubt, and clinging to nothing; and who has become cooled—him do I call a Brāhmin.

415. He who, having given up sense pleasures here, has renounced the household life and has become a monk or a nun and has destroyed both cravings for sense pleasures and existence—him do I call a Brāhmin.

416. He who, having given up craving for sense pleasures here, has renounced the household life, has become a monk or a nun, and has destroyed craving and repeated existence—him do I call a Brāhmin.

417. He who, having given up human bondage, and having gone beyond heavenly bondage, is released from all bondage—him do I call a Brāhmin.

418. He who, having given up liking for sense pleasures and disliking for meditation, has become cooled, without defilements, and is a true hero who has conquered all the worlds—him do I call a Brāhmin.

419. He who, in every way knows the passing away and rebirth of beings, is totally detached from all existence, has gone on the path of

Nibbāna, and is enlightened—him do I call a Brāhmin.

420. He whose track no god, no angel, or no human can trace, the liberated one whose impurities are destroyed—him do I call a Brāhmin.

421. He who has no defilements with regard to the past, present and future, who is undefiled and clings to nothing—him do I call a Brāhmin.

422. He who is like the best type of bull, the excellent, the great hero, the great sage, the conqueror of Māra's army, free from craving, has cleansed defilements, and is enlightened—him do I call a Brāhmin.

423. He who remembers his former lives, who sees heaven and hell with his divine eye, who has attained the end of rebirth and attained the higher knowledges, and who has reached the full culmination of spiritual excellence, Nibbāna—him do I call a Brāhmin.

Mahamegha Publications:
Sutta Translations
- Stories of Sakka, Lords of Gods: Sakka Samyutta
- Stories of Brahmas: Brahma Samyutta
- Stories of Heavenly Mansions: Vimanavatthu
- Stories of Ghosts: Petavatthu
- The Voice of Enlightened Monks: The Theragatha
- The Voice of Enlightened Nuns: The Therigatha

Dhamma Books
- Mahamevnawa Pali-English Paritta Chanting Book
- The Wise Shall Realize
- The Life of the Buddha for Children

Children's Picture Books

- Chaththa Manawaka
- Sumana the Novice Monk
- Stingy Kosiya of Town Sakkara
- Kisagothami
- Kali the She-Devil
- Ayuwaddana Kumaraya
- Sumana the Florist
- Sirigutta and Garahadinna
- The Banker Anathapindika

Made in United States
North Haven, CT
11 January 2025